NEW BOOK INFORMATION

BOOKWRIGHT

TITLE: SUMMER

AUTHOR: RALPH WHITLOCK

SERIES: SEASONS

PUBLICATION: MARCH   1987

ISBN: 0-531-18106-5

GRADES: M

BINDING: S&L

PRICE: 11.90

PAGES: 48

VIVIDLY CAPTURES THE IMPORTANT FACTS
ABOUT THE OUTDOOR TIME THAT WE CALL
SUMMER. INCLUDES INFORMATION ON SUMMER
SPORTS THROUGHTOUT THE WORLD, ARRANGING
SUMMER FLOWERS, AND FAMOUS LITERARY AND
ARTISTIC WORKS THAT HAVE ALLUDED TO THE
SEASON.

574

FRANKLIN
Watts
A GROLIER COMPANY
387 Park Avenue South, New York, N.Y. 10016

THE SEASONS

Summer

Ralph Whitlock

The Bookwright Press
New York · 1987

Titles in this series

Spring
Summer

Designed by Malcolm Smythe

First published in the
United States in 1987 by
The Bookwright Press
387 Park Avenue South
New York, NY 10016

ISBN 0–531–18106–5
Library of Congress Catalog Card Number 86–71545

First published in 1986 by
Wayland (Publishers) Ltd
61 Western Road, Hove
East Sussex BN3 1JD, England

© Copyright 1986 Wayland (Publishers) Ltd

Typeset by DP Press Ltd, Sevenoaks
Manufactured in Belgium by Casterman

Contents

What seasons are

In the temperate regions of the world the year divides naturally into four seasons, according to the changing length of day and night and the changing temperature. The four seasons are spring, summer, autumn, or fall, and winter.

It takes many weeks for one season to change into the next. However, there are natural dividing lines between the seasons, called equinoxes and solstices. The equinoxes are the dates on which day and night are of equal length. They occur on March 21 and September 23. The solstices are the dates of the extremes. At the winter solstice the day length is at its shortest and the night length at its longest. The summer solstice has the longest day and the shortest night. In the northern half of the world (the Northern

Summer is the best season for insects, like this burnet moth.

Hemisphere) the winter solstice occurs on December 21 and the summer solstice on June 21. In the southern half of the world (the Southern Hemisphere) the seasons are reversed. This is explained in the table below:

Northern Hemisphere			
Winter	Spring	Summer	Autumn
December	March	June	September
January	April	July	October
February	May	August	November
Summer	Autumn	Winter	Spring
Southern Hemisphere			

Seasons vary in different parts of the world. Near the equator, the climate remains the same all year round and the length of the day never varies. In the rest of the tropics (including Africa, India, Southeast Asia and northern Australia) there are two main seasons. One is hot and wet, the other cooler and dry.

The Arctic has seasons, though its summers are very short. In Antarctica it is cold all the time.

In the temperate regions the four seasons can be clearly defined. However, even here the seasons are not quite the same everywhere. The summers are longer and hotter in temperate areas that are situated nearer the tropics.

Spectacular sunsets add the final touch to long summer evenings.

Why seasons happen

To understand seasons we need to know why they happen. The earth is like a huge ball, spinning through space. We divide the time it takes to complete one spin on its axis into twenty-four hours – one day and one night.

The spinning earth also orbits the sun, taking one year to complete its journey. But there is a complication. The earth is tilted. As a result, the midday sun is directly overhead at different places at different times of the year. For part of the year the earth's Northern Hemisphere is tilted toward the sun, which makes the days longer than the nights. For the rest of the year it is the Southern Hemisphere that faces the sun, and then the southern days are long and the nights short.

Scientists draw an imaginary line around the earth, halfway between the two Poles, and call it the equator. At the equator day and night are always the same length. One quarter of the distance from the equator to the Poles two other imaginary lines are drawn, parallel to the equator. The one north of the equator is called the Tropic of Cancer: the southern one is called the Tropic of Capricorn. The zone between the two is the tropical zone, and the sun is never directly overhead except in this zone.

How sunlight reaches the earth
Different parts of the earth receive different amounts of sunlight. Tropical regions around the equator receive more concentrated sunlight than elsewhere, as they are closest to the sun. The farther away one goes from the equator, the weaker the sunlight becomes because it has to travel farther through the atmosphere. Therefore sunlight is less strong in temperate regions and very weak in polar regions.

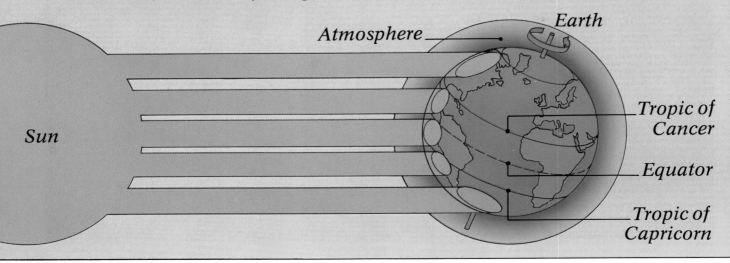

Sun

Atmosphere

Earth

Tropic of Cancer

Equator

Tropic of Capricorn

South Africa lies in the Southern Hemisphere. The climate is mild in winter and very warm in summer.

At the summer solstice in the Northern Hemisphere the sun is directly overhead at the Tropic of Cancer. The countries of the Northern Hemisphere receive many hours of sunshine and have short nights. So it is summer in the North and winter in the South. At the summer solstice in the Southern Hemisphere the sun is directly overhead at the Tropic of Capricorn, so the southern regions have summer while the north is cold and days are short. At the two equinoxes the sun is directly overhead at the equator, and day and night are of equal length in both the Northern and Southern Hemisphere.

Seasonal changes in daylight

The earth orbits the sun once a year. On June 21 (northern midsummer) the sun is directly above the Tropic of Cancer. On December 21 (southern midsummer) it is right over the Tropic of Capricorn. On March 21 and September 23 (the equinoxes) the sun is directly over the equator.

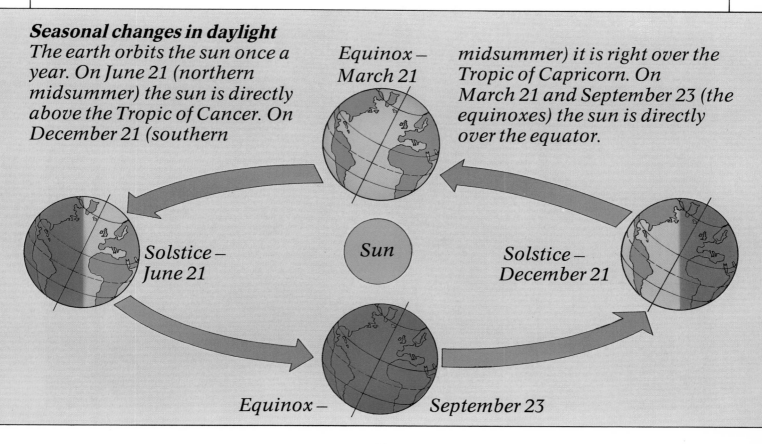

Equinox – March 21

Solstice – June 21

Sun

Solstice – December 21

Equinox – September 23

Summer weather

We have all enjoyed summer days when the warm sun has shone all day long. When the dry, sunny weather continues for long periods, however, it develops into a drought, which is not so pleasant. The temperature rises too high to be comfortable, the soil becomes dry, and plants wither. In some places water shortages occur in most summers. In Australia such droughts often lead to bush fires.

Extreme summer weather occurs most often right in the middle of continents. Often in these regions the change from winter to summer is very abrupt, with hardly any spring in between. Within a week snow lying on the ground melts and temperatures soar to summer levels. It often happens in the Mississippi Valley and the Prairie states, where a warm wind sweeping up from the Gulf of Mexico not only evaporates the snow but creates tornadoes, which do a lot of damage.

Summer weather varies greatly in the temperate regions. Most northern and eastern European countries, New Zealand, eastern Australia, the southeastern United States and Turkey receive even rainfall all year, including summer, but Spain and the Mediterranean countries have very dry, hot summers. In the northern

The snow-capped summit of Mount Kilimanjaro in equatorial Africa.

Droughts often occur in hot parts of Australia. Shown below is parched ground in New South Wales.

United States and Canada, summers are dry but cooler. And in northern Mexico, which is near the tropical zone, it is actually much wetter in summer than in winter.

Altitude also affects the weather. Mount Kilimanjaro in East Africa is less than 400 km (250 miles) from the equator, but its summit is permanently snow-covered because it is so high (5,895 m or 19,340 ft).

In warmer climates violent thunderstorms often occur after long hot periods. Often such thunderstorms are greeted with delight, because they bring much-needed rain to freshen the dry, dusty air.

Northern temperate countries like Britain often have cloudy weather.

Summer around the world

The countries that share the northern summer are most of Europe, (except the far north), the United States, much of Canada, Japan, most of China and much of Russia and Siberia. The chief southern countries that have summer when the northern ones are in their winter are Australia, New Zealand, South Africa, Argentina, Chile and southern Brazil.

In the parts of the temperate zones that are nearest the tropics (such as northern Africa, Mediterranean Europe, Mexico and part of the Middle East) summer comes early. Plants grow quickly after the spring rains, but because of the hot sunshine their flowers are soon over. Very soon the seeds ripen and farmers harvest their crops. There then follows a long period of dry weather when the sun is so hot that everybody rests and sleeps in the midday heat, doing their work in early morning and late evening when it is cooler. This midday rest is called a siesta.

In the intermediate temperate zones summer is more gentle and less dramatic. In some countries, such as Australia, summer conditions vary

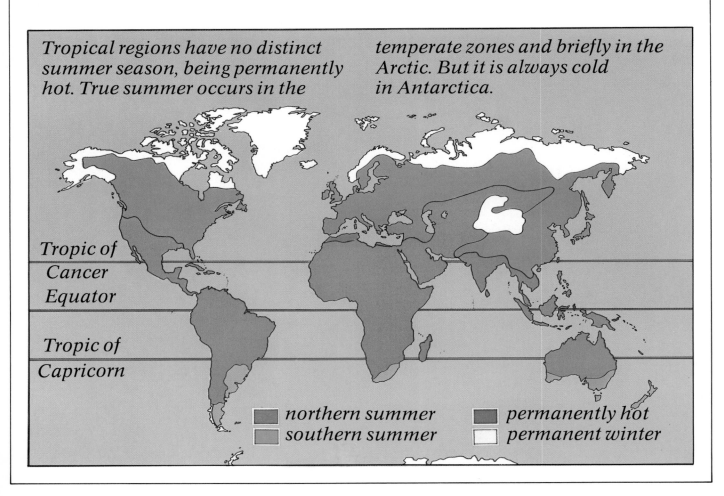

Tropical regions have no distinct summer season, being permanently hot. True summer occurs in the temperate zones and briefly in the Arctic. But it is always cold in Antarctica.

Tropic of Cancer
Equator
Tropic of Capricorn

northern summer
southern summer
permanently hot
permanent winter

greatly. The northern part is tropical, while the southern part is temperate.

In the parts of the temperate zones nearest the polar regions, such as Alaska, northern Canada, northern Scandinavia and Siberia, summer comes late. Snowstorms and frost often occur even as late as the summer solstice. The soil takes a long time to warm up after having been frozen throughout the long winter. However, the brief Arctic summer is spectacular.

In the high Arctic the summer lasts only about six weeks, but it is always daylight. The sun seems to perform a great circle in the sky, never setting. The Arctic is then a scene of hectic activity, for nature has to fit its breeding and growing period into those few weeks. Flowers bloom in profusion and millions of birds nest on the shores of lakes and rivers. Insects multiply there too — mosquitoes are as plentiful and troublesome as they are in the tropics. The Antarctic, however, is so cold that it never has a real summer, even when the sun is visible all day and all night. It is like a permanent refrigerator.

The Arctic tern visits the Arctic in summer to breed.

Wildlife in summer

In temperate climates most creatures are born in the spring. That gives them all summer to grow and mature and acquire sufficient skill to find their own food in the coming winter. Most young birds and animals stay with their parents for some weeks or months after birth, gradually learning to fend for themselves. Many adult birds produce two or even three broods of young during the spring and summer. With some birds, such as swallows, the young adults of the first brood help to feed those of the later broods.

Young birds and animals need not only warmth and sunshine, but plenty of food. Grazing animals, such as deer,

Rabbits are a familiar sight in the country during the summer.

The mandarin duck from birth to adult

Ducklings hatch in spring. They are born covered with fluffy down. Unlike baby birds, ducklings do not depend totally on the adult birds for food.

Very soon after they are born, ducklings learn to swim. They follow their mother, feeding on floating insects and water weed. By summer they are young adults.

The young adult's plumage is often different from the mature adult's. Compare the young mandarin duck (left) with the adult (below).

Duckling

Young adult

Mature adult

In late summer large numbers of caribou begin their long southward journey to escape the harsh winters of the north.

antelopes and cattle, eat grass and other plants that grow quickly during the summer. So do smaller animals such as rabbits, mice and ground squirrels. Carnivorous animals, such as wolves, foxes, lynxes and weasels, prey on the young birds and animals that are being produced in such abundance. So do predatory birds, such as hawks, crows and many kinds of gulls. Insect-eating birds and animals feed on the insects that are hatching in enormous numbers all through the summer.

In late summer, when the breeding season is over, birds shed their feathers and grow a new set. This process is known as molting. Many animals, too, especially deer, shed their coats and horns, or antlers, and grow new ones.

In summer many birds and animals tend to collect in flocks. The process usually starts as one or two families join together when they go looking for food. For many birds and animals it is good practice for migration. Swallows, geese and caribou (a kind of reindeer) often collect in large flocks or herds for their long journey southward, to escape the northern winter. They usually put on a lot of weight before they start out, the fat being used up as fuel on the exhausting southward journey.

Flowers in summer

Summer flowers come into bloom when all danger of frost and snow has passed, and when the winds are not so violent. So, unlike the low-growing, robust spring plants, summer flowers are generally more delicate and often have taller stems. Think of a sturdy spring tulip and compare it with a flimsy summer poppy, swaying in the breeze.

In northern countries flowers can normally rely on about three months before the first frost of autumn occurs. This gives plants enough time to produce flowers and seeds. The sole purpose of their brightly colored flowers, or sweet scent, is to attract insects to pollinate them so seeds may be produced.

The natural short flowering season of summer plants is a problem for plant breeders, who produce new varieties of lovely garden flowers. Every gardener likes to have flowers that keep blooming all through the summer. So plant breeders tend to choose plants that produce a succession of blooms throughout the summer, even though individual blooms do not last long. Roses, sweet peas, cornflowers, marigolds, nasturtiums, sweet williams and fuchsias are some popular summer garden flowers. If you have a garden, or even a windowbox, you can grow your own garden or wild flowers from seeds that you can buy from a garden center or seed catalog.

Summer wild flowers are very interesting and varied. Unlike spring flowers, few summer flowers bloom in woods because the canopy of leaves from the trees blocks out the light. Those that do grow in woods spring up very rapidly, each plant competing with its neighbor for light and space. Meadows, riverbanks, waysides and even areas near the ocean are good places to find wild flowers. If you live in a big town and do not have a garden, you can often find flower borders in parks and public gardens. You can see plenty of wild flowers in towns too – vacant lots may be filled with colorful weeds and wild flowers like ragwort, golden rod and daisies.

A mass of scented roses must be one of the loveliest sights.

How a flower is pollinated

The purpose of all flowers is to be pollinated, mostly by insects, and produce seed.

The bright petals serve to attract insects to the flower. Inside, as the insect gathers nectar, it brushes against male pollen grains, which fall onto the insect. The pollen grains rub off onto the female stigma and in time seeds will form.

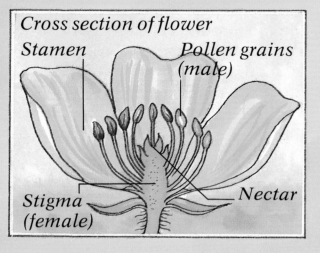

Cross section of flower

Stamen

Pollen grains (male)

Stigma (female)

Nectar

These wild flowers add a bright splash of color to a barley field.

Scented sweet peas will bloom for many weeks during summer.

Insects in summer

Summer is the main season when insects reproduce, just like animals, birds and flowers. The lives of most insects are divided into four stages. These are egg, larva, pupa, or chrysalis, and mature adult. Many insects spend winter (or dry season in hot countries) in the egg or pupa stage. In spring the insect becomes a larva, and in summer it becomes the mature adult.

Insects live in every possible environment. Some live under Antarctic ice, some within the bodies of other living creatures, some even in pools of oil. Probably the most numerous, however, are those that feed on plants.

Someone has calculated that for every human in the world, there are at least a million insects. If all the eggs of a single pair of flies were to survive till the end of summer, there would be

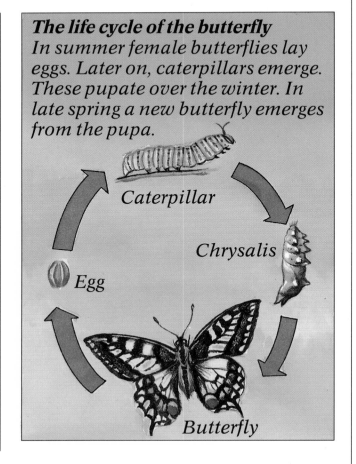

The life cycle of the butterfly
In summer female butterflies lay eggs. Later on, caterpillars emerge. These pupate over the winter. In late spring a new butterfly emerges from the pupa.

Caterpillar

Chrysalis

Egg

Butterfly

How a cricket sheds its skin

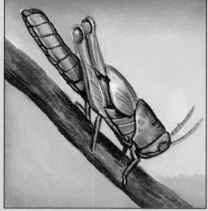

A young cricket has no wings and its skin will not grow.

So, as a cricket grows, it must shed its old tight skin.

It hangs upside down on a stalk and loosens its skin.

several billions of them. Of course, they do not all survive, because insects are food for many kinds of creatures, from birds and animals to spiders and other insects. Even so, by summer's end, even in the Arctic, insects are everywhere.

Summer is the season when insects in the mature, or adult, stage are most plentiful. Their sole function is to breed. Summer therefore sees the countryside alive with courting and mating insects. It is also the time when insects, such as butterflies, lay their eggs, from which larvae will emerge next spring. Some of the loveliest insects, such as butterflies, damselflies and dragonflies are also fairly common and are quite easy to find in the countryside. On sunny days you can find butterflies in meadows, while dragonflies prefer riverbanks.

The impressive swallowtail butterfly of Europe and North America.

When the newly formed cricket breaks out of its old dry skin.

It rests on a stalk to dry its moist skin and new wings.

When it is ready, the perfect new cricket flies away.

Farm animals in summer

Summer is a pleasant season for farm animals, as well as for us. Most of them enjoy the warm sunshine and plenty of food. This is especially true when the animals can roam freely over large areas of land, as on ranches in the United States, Australia, South Africa and South America. Freedom to roam enables them to seek shelter from the hot sun and to take a drink whenever they need to.

Two types of farm animals are not so contented with summer. Pigs have no thick hair or fur to protect them from the sun and so suffer severely from sunburn if they cannot find shade. Best of all, they like a muddy pool to wallow in. Sheep are mountain animals and grow very thick coats of wool, known as fleece, to protect them from the frost and blizzards of winter. In summer wild sheep retreat up the mountains toward the cooler snow line. Farm sheep cannot do this, and so at the beginning of summer the farmer shears off their thick winter fleece. The wool from the sheep is an important farm product and is sold to factories for weaving into clothes. Sheep shearing is regarded as a kind of

Summer is a busy time for farm workers on large cattle ranches.

festival in some countries, such as Wales and New Zealand. Farming families gather to help each other with the shearing and afterward join together to have a feast.

In the cooler parts of the temperate zones, such as Britain, New Zealand, northern Europe, Canada and northern United States, as well as southern South America, farmers have the problem of conserving some of the spring grass to feed their animals during the winter. One popular method is to cut the grass just as it is beginning to flower, dry it and then store it as hay. Another is to cut it a bit earlier, when it is still mostly leaf, and compress it to form silage. The animals cannot, of course, be allowed to trample on grass that is being kept for that purpose, so in well-settled countries fences have to be erected to prevent them from staying.

Among the chief irritations for animals during the summer are the stinging and biting insects, which are plentiful at this time of year. On hot summer days you will often see cattle and horses swishing their tails, as they try to shake off flies and other pests.

Rounding up time on an Australian sheep farm.

The farmer's summer crops

For the farmer the climax of the summer is the harvest. During the early summer farmers watch their crops growing, then ripening, until at last they are ripe enough to be gathered for use. When we speak of harvest we generally mean the gathering of various types of grain, such as wheat, barley, rye, sweet corn and rice. Unlike what happens with hay, these crops, known as cereals, are allowed to continue growing after the flowering stage. Just like hay, these cereals are actually grasses; they produce seed that is allowed to ripen and is then collected to make bread and other types of foods. This has been the practice for the past 6,000 years at least.

Below In temperate countries wheat is often harvested in midsummer.

The harvest is gathered by cutting the standing plant, now dry and brown, and threshing out the grain. This may be done by the combine harvester, a machine that cuts and threshes the grain at the same time. Where the grain is grown in terraces, on steep hillsides, or where people cannot afford to buy a combine harvester, it is cut by hand, using a sickle or scythe. The grain is threshed later on.

In the northern temperate zone, crops naturally ripen early nearest the southern edge, adjoining the tropics. The harvest then progresses north. In the United States contractors with combine harvesters are able to begin work on the harvest near the Mexican border in June and July and follow the harvest northward, finishing up in Canada in October or even November.

Farmers need fine weather for harvesting and, therefore, heavy rain in the summer can be very frustrating for farmers. But they need water as well to keep the crops growing in the months before harvest and sometimes rainfall is insufficient. When this happens, the crops have to be irrigated. In Egypt for example rainfall is scarce, and the crops are watered by irrigation channels from the Nile River.

Opposite In Indonesia rice is grown during the wet season and harvested in the dry season.

Fruit, vegetables and other crops

Grass can be considered a farm crop, like wheat and rice. Throughout the summer it is harvested at intervals, sometimes by animals grazing it and sometimes by machines, which make it into hay or silage. After each crop of grass is taken, the plants have to be encouraged to make new growth by applying fertilizers and, if necessary, by watering.

Apart from grass, the earliest harvest in countries with a temperate climate is of strawberries, which ripen in early summer. A few weeks later raspberries, red and black currants, gooseberries and loganberries, which are known as soft fruits, are picked. Plums ripen in

A lemon grove in Sicily with fruit ready for harvest. Citrus fruits grow well in Mediterranean lands.

A grove of olive trees with ripe fruit in Greece.

mid to late summer, and apples and pears a little later.

Peaches, nectarines and apricots are abundant in the countries around the Mediterranean. Citrus fruits, such as oranges, lemons and grapefruit, are also plentiful there and in parts of the world with similar climates, such as California and Florida, and countries near the tropics such as Australia and South Africa. Olives, from which olive oil is extracted, are also a Mediterranean crop, growing in Greece, southern France and Italy.

Certain crops can ripen only in those regions that have an even hotter summer. Sugarcane, tobacco, cotton, bananas, pineapples, coconuts and coffee will grow only in countries with hot, dry summers, such as the southern United States and parts of India, Australia, South America and South Africa. In these countries, such crops are very important. These warm countries also grow more cereal crops, including millet and sorghum, which need very hot summers in order to ripen.

Tea needs a moderately temperate climate but is successfully grown in the cooler mountain regions of otherwise tropical countries, such as India, Kenya and Sri Lanka, rather than in the temperate zone.

Pineapples can be grown in the hotter part of Australia.

Summer festivals, old and new

In the Northern Hemisphere religious festivals are generally not as numerous in summer as in spring. However, it was an ancient practice to celebrate the summer solstice, and huge monuments were built aligned to the sunrise. At the ancient stone circle at Stonehenge in England, some people still celebrate the summer solstice each year. Bonfires played an important part in some Midsummer ceremonies.

Midsummer was also formerly considered to be a dangerous time, when ghosts and spirits prowled about at night. So Midsummer Eve was a "watch night" or "wake night" when people stayed awake all night.

The summer feast of Corpus Christi is important to Roman Catholics. Colorful processions are led by clergy, plays are performed on temporary stages, and there is a festive, lively atmosphere. In June or July many European countries hold summer fairs or festivals. In Spain, such occasions are called Fiesta.

In the Southern Hemisphere, for example in Australia, South America and New Zealand, Christmas falls in summertime and may even be celebrated on the beach. A date of special importance to Americans is Independence Day, the Fourth of July. This day is celebrated with parades and fireworks displays.

Druids assembled around the stone circle at Stonehenge to celebrate the summer solstice.

Summer celebrations in Minorca during the Fiesta.

Jewish, Muslim and Buddhist festivals

The farther south one goes in the Northern Hemisphere, and the farther north in the Southern Hemisphere, the earlier the harvest ripens. Therefore, although in Britain, northern Europe and much of North America harvest festivals are held in the autumn, in warmer countries they are summer events.

The Jewish harvest festival is the feast of Pentecost, or Shavuot, which falls in early summer. This festival honors the giving of the Ten Commandments to Moses. Synagogues are specially decorated with flowers and plants for the occasion, and a family feast is held.

In late summer, (September or October) the Jews celebrate the Feast of Tabernacles, or Succoth, which is the Festival of the Fruit Harvest. A tabernacle (or *succah*) is a temporary tent or hut with an open roof. In the past the Jewish people lived in such temporary dwellings when they were away from home, gathering fruit. Tabernacles also hold a special significance for Jewish people as a reminder of the days when their ancestors spent forty years wandering in the wilderness and living in tents. Nowadays during the Feast, Jewish families construct a simple *succah* in their garden. This is made of a latticework of wood with a slatted roof of bamboo or fine branches. Meals are eaten in the *succah* and families sometimes sleep there.

A Succoth celebration in Israel.

26

Some Arabs and Indians have traditional ceremonies in which they return to the soil samples of the crops they have taken from it.

Muslims celebrate the summer festival of *Milad-an-Nabi*. This remembers the birthday of the Prophet Muhammad, who was born on a date corresponding to August 20, AD 560. Every year bright processions take place in Muslim countries in honor of this occasion.

In Sri Lanka the Buddhist festival *Esala Perahera*, which falls in midsummer, is an occasion of great festivity. On the night of the full moon in August there is a huge torchlit procession in the city of Kandy. A long line of people and decorated elephants process through the streets, and the sacred tooth of the Buddha is carried in a golden casket on the back of a huge elephant. The whole procession is a spectacular sight.

The torchlit procession of Esala Perahera *in Kandy, Sri Lanka.*

Summer sports

Summer sports are naturally played outdoors. In the United States baseball is a very popular sport — in fact it is called the national pastime. The game requires warm summer weather to be enjoyable, for many players have to spend long periods standing in the field or sitting in the dugout, and many Big League games are played at night, under lights. Baseball is popular also in Japan, Canada and the Caribbean Islands. To the fans sitting in the bleachers, and to players of all ages from Little Leaguers to Old Timers, "baseball" means "summer."

An international test match in progress in Calcutta, India.

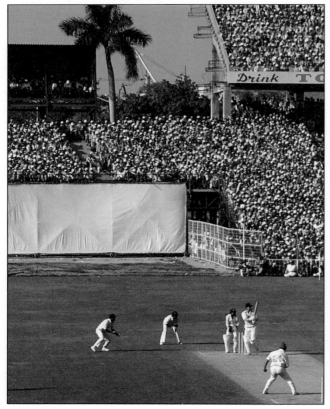

In England, Australia, India, Pakistan and the West Indies, cricket replaces baseball as a popular summer sport and attracts just as much enthusiasm on the part of the spectators. Originally cricket and baseball were probably very much the same game, being ball games without many rules played on village greens in England. Baseball may originally have come from the English game of "rounders," although the American version of the game was invented in 1839 in Cooperstown, New York, by Abner Doubleday.

Tennis is a very popular summer sport. International tennis matches around the world are watched by thousands of enthusiastic fans in the stands and on television.

Badminton is another outdoor sport played with rackets, but uses a special shuttlecock. This "ball" used to be made of feathers.

Golf, although not exclusively a summer sport, is most enjoyable when played in the warm summer weather. Outdoor athletic gatherings have become increasingly popular in recent years.

Many people enjoy water sports. Swimming in the ocean is always pleasant, but more exhilarating are the demanding sports of windsurfing and water skiing. Both at the ocean and on inland waters, there are regattas, speedboat racing, rowing and canoeing.

Above *Windsurfing has become increasingly popular in recent years.*

Below *A baseball game in Chicago.*

Summer recreations

Summer is the season for enjoying recreation in the town or countryside and, perhaps, for going on a vacation.

Children on vacation like water and sand and when they grow up, many of them regard the beach as the best place for a vacation. As well as being ideal for swimming and sunbathing, the beach is a good place for finding fascinating shellfish. Some children collect the attractive pebbles or seashells they find.

But the beach is not the only place for a vacation. There are, for instance, camping, walking, fishing and adventure vacations. In the United States and Canada summer camps are very popular. These are often organized by schools and include instruction in various outdoor activities, such as rock climbing, canoeing, swimming and tackling obstacle courses.

If you have a camera, summer is a wonderful time for taking photographs. You can keep a photographic record of nature at its brightest, and take pictures of games with your friends, or to remind you of your vacations.

If you live far away from the country, summer can still be fun in the town. Many people enjoy a picnic in the local park. Often there are public tennis courts or outdoor swimming pools for people to use in summer. If there is a lake in your local park, it may be possible for you to go boating there

The white sands of Coogee beach, Sydney, Australia.

Fine summer evenings are ideal for outdoor barbecues. Food cooked in the open tastes especially good.

with an adult.

However, if you are able to go to the country in the summer, you can enjoy seeing many wild flowers, insects and birds. If you are going to a stream, perhaps take a fishing pole or a net with you.

A good way to enjoy a fine summer evening is an outdoor barbecue. In parts of Australia barbecues and parties are often held on the beach, as they are in the United States.

Some theater companies put on outdoor plays on summer evenings. Shakespeare's "A Midsummer Night's Dream" is an ideal choice. You might like to get together with your friends to perform an outdoor play — perhaps one you have written yourself.

Some fishing trips result in a good catch.

Summer clothes

For many people, especially the young, summer means freedom. It is not only the season of long vacations but a season when we can discard our heavy winter clothes and let our bodies feel the sun. In winter when we want to go outdoors we have to dress in thick clothes (unless we are going jogging or playing energetic games). In Northern Hemisphere countries people need to wear coats, hats, scarves and gloves, and rubber boots. Getting ready to go outside is a complicated, lengthy affair.

How free we feel, when summer comes, to be able to run outside with the same clothes we are wearing indoors, wearing light shoes, or perhaps nothing at all on our feet. Our clothes are of lighter materials, too. Girls can wear light summer dresses. For casual clothes, boys and girls can wear T-shirts and shorts. Sometimes we can lie in the hot sun, wearing just a bathing suit.

We should remember, though, that the summer sun has its dangers. We may need to wear sunglasses to protect our eyes from the glare. In very hot weather a sunhat is advisable. For fair-skinned people, especially, suntan lotions are a valuable protection against sunburn.

Have you noticed that people who live in hot countries, such as Arabs of the Middle East, wear long, flowing robes that cover most of their bodies? They do so because these clothes help

In fine summer weather it is warm enough to wear shorts all day long.

to keep out the intense heat. Their clothes are usually white or of some other bright color, because these colors reflect the heat. Dark colors absorb the heat and are therefore much warmer to wear.

Natural fabrics, especially cotton, absorb moisture and so are ideal to wear in hot weather. T-shirts, for example, are usually made of knitted cotton jersey, which is why they are so comfortable. Nylon and other synthetic fabrics tend to be rather hot in summer because, being densely woven, they do not readily let body heat escape. However, nylon is often used for bathing suits because it dries quickly. Synthetic fabrics are also used for lightweight raincoats that protect against summer showers.

Left *Light clothing leaves us free to move when playing games.*

Below *Tunisia is a country with a hot climate and so the people there wear white to reflect the heat.*

Summer in art and literature

The countryside in summer was one of the earliest themes illustrated in art. The three pictures illustrated here depict summer activities over several different centuries. The picture of peasants shearing sheep in summertime (top left) was painted in medieval times. Notice how green the trees are — clearly this picture was painted in early summer, before the leaves change color.

Shown top right is a picture by George Stubbs (1724–1806) of farm workers loading new hay onto a cart. Although this picture is beautifully painted, it is not a realistic scene of haymaking 200 years ago — the workers are certainly better dressed than they would have been at that time.

More recent still is the picture by the French impressionist painter, Claude Monet. Painted in 1872, *Wild Poppies* captures the mood of a breezy midsummer's day in the country. Clouds are racing along against the blue sky. The ladies are wearing straw hats and carrying parasols to keep off the heat of the sun. In the field of long summer grass, a mass of scarlet poppies are gently swaying in the breeze.

Gifted authors have been able to recapture the same summery

Claude Monet's picture Wild Poppies *captures a perfect summer's day.*

A medieval picture of sheep shearing in the green countryside of early summer.

George Stubbs painted this scene of haymaking in rural England in the eighteenth century.

atmosphere. Here is Mark Twain depicting Tom Sawyer's hometown on a Saturday morning in summer:

"All the summer world was bright and fresh, and brimming with life. There was a song in every heart . . . . There was a cheer in every face, and a spring in every step. The locust trees were in bloom, and the fragrance of the blossoms filled the air."

Below Mark Twain describes the midday heat in summer:

"It was the sleepiest of sleepy days . . . Away off in the flaming sunshine Cardiff Hill lifted its soft green sides through a shimmering veil of heat tinted with the purple of distance; a few birds floated on the lazy wind high in the air; no other living thing was visible but some cows, and they were asleep."

In his nineteenth-century book *The Mayor of Casterbridge*, the English writer Thomas Hardy describes a warm, late summer morning:

"The morning sun was streaming through the crevices of the canvas when the man awoke. A warm glow pervaded the whole atmosphere of the marquee, and a single big blue fly buzzed musically round and round it. Besides the buzz of the fly there was not a sound."

Summer in songs, sayings and verse

One of the earliest and best-known songs about summer is English. It looks forward to summertime:

Summer is icumen in
Lhude sing cuccu!

The song tells of spring growth but the writer believes that when the cuckoo sings loudly in spring, he is waiting for summer.

Some hymns also describe the heat and brightness of summer:

Summer suns are glowing
Over land and sea,
Happy light is flowing
Bountiful and free.
Everything rejoices
In the mellow rays . . .

Poets, especially, like to write about summer. In his poem "The Scholar Gypsy," Matthew Arnold describes the beauty of high summer. As you read this extract, imagine the sights, sounds and scents which the poet mentions:

. . . Here will I sit and wait,
While to my ear from uplands
  far away
The bleating of the folded
  flocks is borne,
With distant cries of reapers in
  the corn —
All the live murmurs of summer's
  day.

Screen'd is this nook o'er high,
  half-reap'd field,
And here till sun-down shepherd
  will I be!
Through the thick corn the scarlet
  poppies peep,
And round green roots and
  yellowing stalks I see
Pale blue convolvulus in tendrils
  creep;
And air-swept lindens yield
Their scent, and rustle down their
  perfumed showers
Of bloom on the bent grass where
  I am laid,
And bower me from the August
  sun with shade;
And the eye travels down to
  Oxford's towers.

The Australian poet, Dorothea McKellar, describes the joy of the sea in her poem "Bathing Rhyme":

Turquoise-green the laughing sea
And the beach is ivory,
Creamy-yellow, creamy-smooth
How those small waves lisp
  and soothe!
. . . There's no soul for many a mile
And the curved waves call and
  smile . . .
Quick, your garments cast aside
Go to meet the rising tide!

Summer sayings include "One swallow doesn't make a summer" and "In August it rains honey and wine."

The beauty of nature in summer has inspired many writers.

Things to do – Looking at nature

It is a good idea to keep a nature diary, noting down the changes that occur during the year. In summer new flowers are coming into bloom each day, new butterflies are flying and young birds are being fed by busy parents.

Wherever you are, keep a note of the wild flowers you find. Unless the flower is very common do not pick it. Why not draw it or take a photograph? Carry a pocket-sized guidebook to help you to identify the flowers you find. When trying to identify a plant, it is useful to ask yourself some questions. How many petals does the flower have, and what color and shape are they? What are the leaves like?

On summer days many butterflies are on the wing. Using a guidebook, notice the differences between males and females of the same species. Which are more colorful? Which plants do they choose?

Night is the time for observing moths. If you have a garden with scented flowers and shrubs, many moths will be attracted to them. To encourage them to visit, paint a light sugar solution onto the branches of a shrub. Place a lamp or flashlight nearby and stand quietly to watch. If you are lucky, quite a few moths will visit the bush. They are also attracted to the light and you may be able to see them clearly with the lamp. If you want to identify them indoors, catch them with a large net and put them in a jar. Be very careful — even gentle handling will rub off the scales on their wings. When you have recorded the species name, let the moths go immediately.

You may come across caterpillars feeding on weeds or cabbage leaves. If there are plenty of them, you could keep a few in a wooden box with a nylon or metal mesh cover and a floor of soil. Feed them on their favorite leaves every day.

During the summer, full-grown caterpillars will pupate. Early next summer the chrysalis will hatch. Carefully hide the new butterfly or moth under a leaf. When it is ready, it will fly away.

Attracting moths at night

Summer is a good time to observe birds. In late summer watch birds preparing to migrate. Groups of swallows sit on telegraph wires before starting their journey. Binoculars help you to see distant birds. Make a rough sketch of new birds you see, as shown below. Then identify them using a good guidebook.

Some useful birdwatching equipment

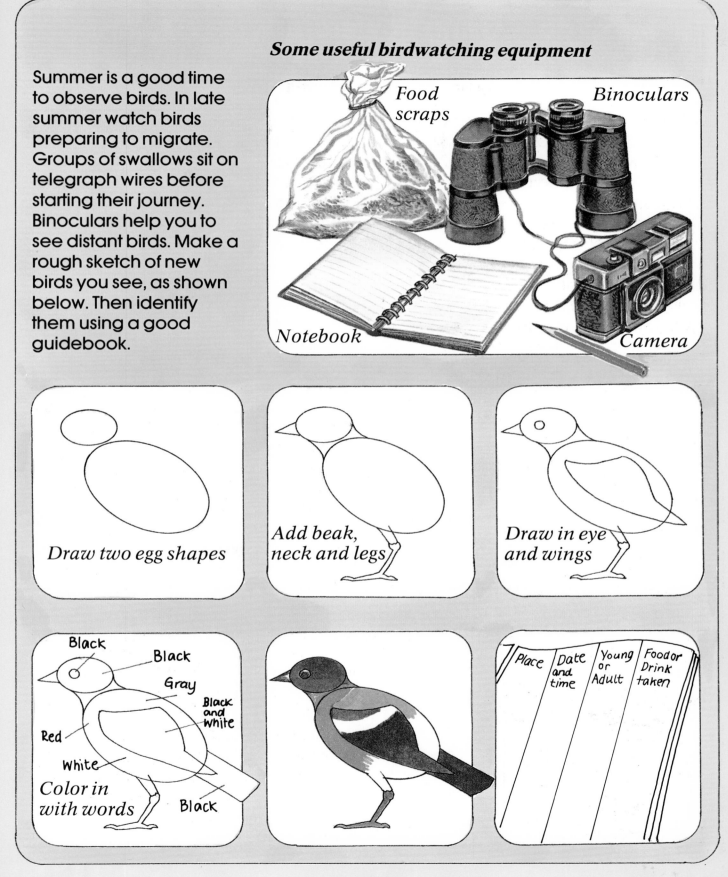

Food scraps

Binoculars

Notebook

Camera

Draw two egg shapes

Add beak, neck and legs

Draw in eye and wings

Black
Black
Gray
Black and white
Red
White
Color in with words
Black

Place | Date and time | Young or Adult | Food or Drink taken

Things to do – Using flowers

One way to keep flowers is by pressing them. Pick richly colored flowers like pansies or poppies. Place them between two sheets of tracing paper and put several heavy books on top. Leave this for a month.

To make a bookmark glue some pressed flowers onto a strip of cardboard and cover both sides with transparent tape. For a greeting card, fold some cardboard in two and glue flowers onto the front.

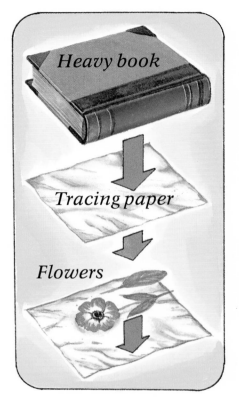

Heavy book

Tracing paper

Flowers

Card

Dried flower

Glue

Dried flowers or grasses make lovely winter decorations. Most dried flowers and grasses fade to an attractive pale blond color. Flowering grasses, ears of wheat, corn stalks, hydrangeas and baby's breath are ideal for drying. The flowers of larkspur (blue or pink) and Chinese lanterns (orange) retain their color when dried.

Gather young flowers and grasses. Tie ones with longer stems into

Foil decoration

Dried flowers

small bundles. Hang these upside down in a dry, airy room or shed. Dry smaller grasses and flowers flat on a tray. Keep them out of strong sunlight.

After several weeks they should be really dry. Arrange the flowers and grasses in simple vases. Or glue flowers and leaves onto a disk of card covered with foil. Make a small hole in the disk, thread some ribbon through and hang up as a decoration.

Why not make a potpourri? This is a fragrant blend of dried flower petals, buds and herbs that have been treated to preserve their scent. Gather the flowers and leaves while fresh and spread out one layer of petals at a time to dry on a tray placed out of direct sunlight. As they dry, and as you add more leaves and petals, sprinkle with a little uniodized salt.

When the mixture has fully dried, add ¼ oz of spices, such as cinnamon, mace, powdered cloves and crushed coriander. Also add a little gum benzoin or storax, which you can obtain from a drugstore. Put the mixture in a jar with a tight-fitting lid and keep sealed for at least a month. Then put the potpourri in bowls to add scent to rooms, or use to fill cloth bags or sachets.

Rose petals, lavender sage, violets, and scented geranium leaves are all good for making potpourri.

The ingredients for potpourri

Drying the petals   *Adding spices*

Displaying

Things to do – summer recipes

On hot summer days we all enjoy a refreshing cold drink. Here is a drink called *Sharbatee Gulab*. Pluck off the petals of five roses, pour 2 quarts cold water over them and stand this in a cool, dark place for four hours. Strain off the petals and add the water to 1½ cups sugar dissolved in ¼ cup lemon juice. Add 3 cups of crushed pineapple and stir well. Pour this over crushed ice and decorate with rose petals.

Milkshakes are very easy to make. For each person, use three-quarters of a large glass of milk. Flavor with fruit syrups or use chocolate powder or coffee. To make a thicker, richer, milkshake add some ice cream.

To mix the drink, place the ingredients in a large, screw-top jar. Seal the lid tightly and shake vigorously for one minute until the ingredients are well mixed and frothy. Pour into tall glasses and serve with straws.

Pouring cold water onto petals

Adding pineapple

Sharbatee Gulab

To bring out the subtle rose flavor, pick the freshest, most fragrant rose petals. If fresh roses are not available, you can use rose water.

Milkshakes

Vanilla ice cream goes well with any flavoring, but you can use flavored ice cream that matches your syrup. It is best not to mix two flavors.

Mix milk and syrup

Shake well and serve

You might want to make a salad. You can mix together almost any kinds of vegetables you like. First wash all ingredients. If you are using lettuce, pick off each leaf and wash separately. Scrub celery stalks well. Next ask an adult to chop or slice all the ingredients for you. Arrange them in a large bowl — wooden or glass bowls make salads look very attractive. Serve with salad dressing or mayonnaise.

Besides vegetables, some fruit and even nuts make excellent salad ingredients. One recipe that is delicious and easy to make is Waldorf salad. For this you need:

  3 eating apples
  4 celery stalks
  2–3 oz chopped
    walnuts
  3–4 oz seedless raisins
  Mayonnaise to taste
  To prepare the salad, wash the apples and celery. Ask an adult to chop these up. Mix well with the raisins and walnuts and stir in the mayonnaise.

Preparing Waldorf salad

Making fruit salads

You can use fruits for dessert salads. Clean the fruit and ask an adult to chop it up. Mix together, adding some water or fruit juice.

The fruits

Choose several different colored fruits. Oranges, bananas, strawberries, cherries, kiwi fruit, grapes and pears are all good in fruit salads.

Fruits for fruit salad

Glossary

Altitude   Height above sea level.

Binoculars   An instrument consisting of two small telescopes joined together. It is used with both eyes. It is useful for viewing distant wildlife.

Cancer   The northern of the two tropics; the sun is directly overhead at this tropic in midsummer (June 21) in the Northern Hemisphere.

Capricorn   The southern of the two tropics, where the sun is directly overhead at midsummer (December 21) in the Southern Hemisphere.

Carnivorous   Flesh-eating.

Chrysalis (or pupa)   The third stage in an insect's life, when it prepares to change from a larva into a mature adult. It is now wrapped in a protective hard skin.

Corpus Christi   Roman Catholic festival. It occurs on the Thursday after Trinity Sunday, which is the Sunday after Pentecost.

Combine harvester   A machine for cutting and theshing grain in one operation.

Equator   An imaginary line around the center of the earth, located midway between the two poles.

Equinox   The day that occurs twice a year when day and night are of equal length.

Fleece   A sheep's coat of wool.

Hemisphere   Half of the earth, as divided by the equator.

Irrigation   Supplying water to growing plants by artificial means.

Larva   The second stage of an insect's life, occurring between the egg and the chrysalis. At this stage the insect takes the form of a "grub" or caterpillar.

Mating   The joining of male and female animals so that they can produce young.

Midsummer   The peak of summer.

Migration   The movement of a group of birds or animals from one part of the world to another at particular times of the year.

Molting   The shedding of feathers or fur, to be replaced by a new coat.

Northern Hemisphere   The half of the earth that is above the equator.

North Pole   The most northerly point on the earth's axis.

Orbit   This word usually refers to the path of one planet moving around the sun.

Pentecost   A Jewish holiday (Shavuot), which serves as a harvest festival; also a Christian holiday that falls on the seventh Sunday after Easter.

Polar regions   The area of the earth within the Arctic and Antarctic circles.

Pollinate   To fertilize by transferring pollen from one flower to another.

Pupate   To develop from a larva into a pupa or chrysalis.

Siesta   A midday rest in hot climates during summer weather.

Solstices   Days when there is the maximum difference between the length of day and night.

South Pole   The most southerly point

on the earth's axis.

Southern Hemisphere   The half of the earth that is south of the equator.

Summer solstice   The longest day of the year, when the sun is at its highest above the horizon. In the Northern Hemisphere, the sun is at its most northerly point in the sky. In the Southern Hemisphere, the sun reaches its most southerly point.

Synagogue   A Jewish place of worship.

Tabernacle   A temporary building, such as a tent or booth.

Temperate zone   The zone between the Arctic Circle and the Tropic of Cancer, and between the Antarctic Circle and the Tropic of Capricorn.

Thresh   To beat stalks of ripe grain so that the useful grain is separated from the outer husk.

Tropical zone   The equatorial zone between the Tropics of Cancer and Capricorn.

Tornadoes   Small but violent storms formed by whirling winds.

Further reading

Allington, Richard L. *Summer*. Milwaukee, WI: Raintree, 1985.
Allison, Linda. *The Reasons for Seasons: The Great Cosmic Megagalactic Trip Without Moving from Your Chair*. Boston: Little, Brown, 1975.
Borland, Hal. *The Golden Circle: A Book of Months*. New York: Crowell Junior Books, 1977.
Bornstein, Harry. *The Holiday Book*. Washington, D.C.: Gallaudet College Press, 1974.
Brandt, Keith. *Wonders of the Seasons*. Mahwah, NJ: Troll Associates, 1982.
Dobler, Lavinia. *Customs and Holidays Around the World*. New York: Fleet Press, 1962.

Index

Picture Acknowledgments

The publishers would like to thank the following for allowing their photographs to be reproduced in this book: Bruce Coleman Limited 5 (D. and J. Bartlett), 8 (David Austen), 12 (Kim Taylor), 13 (Steven C. Kaufman), 14, 15 right (Eric Crichton), 15 left (Hans Reinhard), 17 (John Markham), 20 (Inigo Everson), 22 below (C.B. Frith), 24 (Bruce Coleman), 25 (Roger Wilmshurst), 27 (Dieter and Mary Plage), 28 (Michael Freeman), 30 (David Goulston), 37 (Hans Reinhard), inset cover photograph; E.T. Archive 34, 35 right; Geoscience Features Picture Library 9 below, 11; ZEFA 4 (Dr. David Corke), 8 (Bamm), 21 (Hoffmann-Burchardi), 22 above (K. Herbig), 23 (G. Ricatro), 26, 29 above (Rosenbaum), 29 below (S. Dauner), 31 (C. Voigt), 32 (Schneiders), 33 inset (R. Bond), 33 main picture, main cover photograph. All the illustrations are by Ron Hayward Associates